Coventry
Hidden In Plain Sight

First published in Great Britain in 2009 by The Breedon Books Publishing Company Limited,
Breedon House, 3 The Parker Centre, Derby, DE21 4SZ.

Please see the list of references at the back of the book used for research.
Contact: Clare.Selley@xarra.com

Front cover: *Self Sacrifice (Lady Godiva)* was designed by Edwin Lutyens and sculpted by William Reid-Dick.
Unveiled in 1949, it is cast from bronze.
Previous page: A 19th-century version of the Coventry coat of arms on the façade of the old fire station.
Right: *Broadgate Standard* was unveiled at the entrance to the Upper Precinct in 1948. Covered with gold
leaf, it was created by various industries in Coventry and represents the skill and regeneration of the city.
Back cover: *Flying Cross* by Geoffrey Clarke surmounts the new St Michael's Cathedral's spire.

ISBN 978-1-85983-768-9
Printed and bound by Gutenberg Press Ltd, Malta.

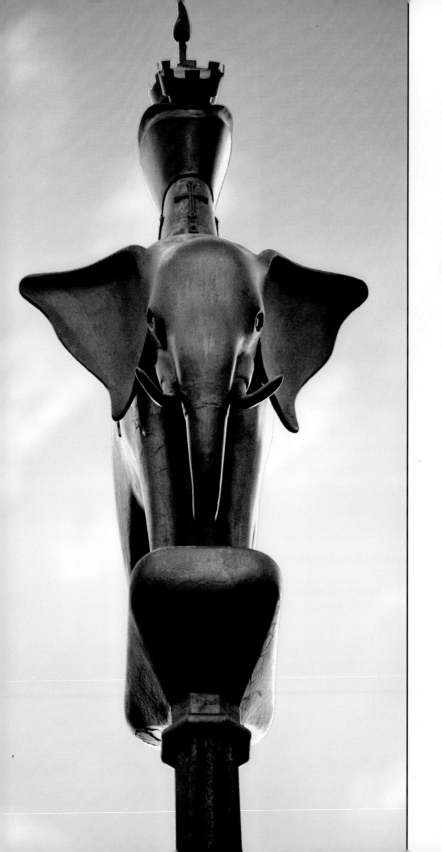

Coventry
Hidden In Plain Sight

Clare Selley

breedon **books**
PUBLISHING

Dedication and Thanks

This photobook is dedicated to:

My husband, Ian, for putting up with me monopolising the camera, disappearing all the time to take photographs, and spending all my evenings editing them.

Thank you also to:

David McGrory for his time and expertise ensuring that the historical information is accurate.

The staff at BBC Coventry and Warwickshire for running the My Coventry Project.

Judith Taylor, Rashida Tingle, Peter Walters of CVOne, Mark Twissell of Coventry City Council, and Richard Harrison for their encouragement and assistance.

Above: Carved stone coat of arms within the Council House entrance hall, by Henry Wilson and Garrett and Simster.

Introduction

I have lived in Coventry for about eight years now, and until I started taking photographs for this project I had never noticed even half of the wonderful stonework and art around the city. This photobook was inspired by several photographs I entered into the BBC Coventry and Warwickshire My Coventry project in 2009. I felt they showed the history of Coventry – and the parts of Coventry that should be preserved.

When I discovered SoFoBoMo (Solo Photobook Month) online, I debated taking up the challenge but could not think of a topic until I realised I had a wealth of inspiration on my doorstep, and the Coventry Photobook was born. The rules of SoFoBoMo are simple: complete a photobook from scratch, containing a minimum of 35 photographs taken within a 31-day period between 1 May 2009 and 31 June 2009. While there have been a few changes to the photos within the book, and captions have been added, the majority of the photographs were taken between 18 May and 18 June 2009.

I have probably missed out many interesting locations, and I limited myself to within the ring road as much as possible, in order not to double the size of the book. Even so, I took well over 10,000 photographs around Coventry, and had to edit ruthlessly.

I would like to thank all the locations that allowed me to photograph their buildings and and the staff who showed me details that I would not have normally noticed.

I would also like to thank the Public Monuments and Sculpture Association (www.PMSA.org.uk) for allowing me to reference their database in such detail for the captions. The PMSA database was invaluable for locating names and details of the artwork around Coventry. Rob Orland's Historic Coventry website (www.historiccoventry.co.uk) and Peter Barton's Coventry Pages (www.thecoventrypages.net) were also essential for information about the city, as was Take A Pew (www.take-a-pew.org.uk) for information about Holy Trinity Church.

I hope you enjoy looking at my Coventry and discover some places you never knew existed.

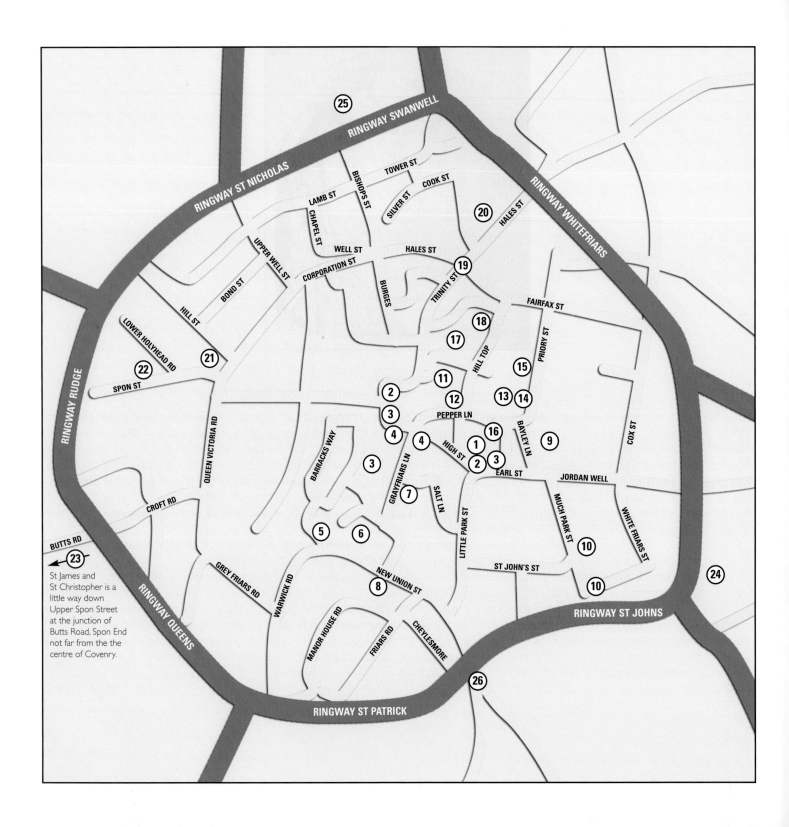

RINGWAY SWANWELL

RINGWAY ST NICHOLAS

RINGWAY WHITEFRIARS

RINGWAY RUDGE

RINGWAY QUEENS

RINGWAY ST JOHNS

RINGWAY ST PATRICK

㉕

TOWER ST
BISHOPS ST
LAMB ST
SILVER ST
COOK ST
CHAPEL ST
HALES ST
㉚
WELL ST
HALES ST
UPPER WELL ST
CORPORATION ST
BURGES
TRINITY ST
㉙
BOND ST
FAIRFAX ST
HILL ST
㉘
LOWER HOLYHEAD RD
㉗ HILL TOP
PRIORY ST
㉑
⑮
㉒
⑪
SPON ST
② ⑫
⑬ ⑭
③ PEPPER LN
QUEEN VICTORIA RD
④
⑯ BAYLEY LN
BARRACKS WAY
④ ① ⑨
③ HIGH ST
② ③
CROFT RD
GRAYFRIARS LN
⑦ SALT LN EARL ST JORDAN WELL
COX ST
③
MUCH PARK ST
⑤ ⑥
LITTLE PARK ST
WHITE FRIARS ST
BUTTS RD
← ㉓
St James and
St Christopher is a
little way down
Upper Spon Street
at the junction of
Butts Road, Spon End
not far from the the
centre of Covenry.
GREY FRIARS RD
NEW UNION ST
ST JOHN'S ST
⑩
⑧
WARWICK RD
⑩
㉔
MANOR HOUSE RD
FRIARS RD
CHEYLESMORE
㉖
RINGWAY ST PATRICK

Contents

Council House

The Council House is richly decorated with heraldry and statues by Henry Wilson and Garrett and Simster, including ones of Justitia, Earl Leofric and the well-known Lady Godiva. Built between 1913 and 1917, with a pause for World War One, the Council House was officially opened by HRH the Duke of York on 11 June 1920.

Above and right: Coventry's civic sword and mace.

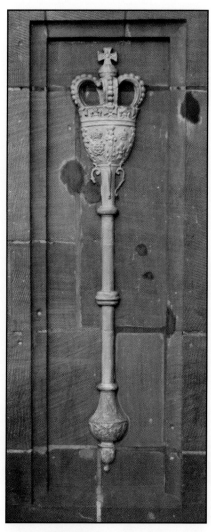

Lady Godiva

Lady Godiva, or Godgifu, was a lady of high status around the 11th century. She is famous for supposedly riding through the city naked, although the term could also refer to her wearing only her shift or stripped of her jewellery, in order to get her husband, Lord Leofric, to stop imposing taxes on the townspeople.

Far left and far right: Statues of Lord Leofric and Lady Godiva.

GODIVA

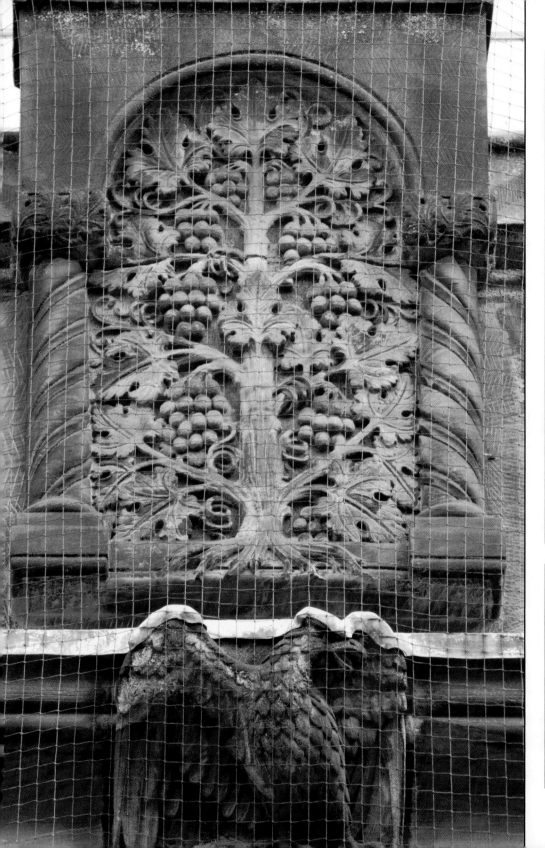

Previous page, left: St Mary's Street and the cathedrals.

Previous page, right: Carved details around the exterior of the Council House.

Left: Carved details from the Council House.

Right: Statue of Justitia.

Above: The entranceway to the Council House is decorated with detailed animals and birds, from hedgehogs and big cats to cockerels and herons.

Right: The Coventry elephant and castle with a cat-a-mountain and city motto.

CAMERA·PRINCIPIS

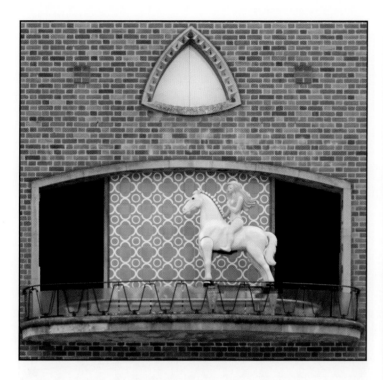

Peeping Tom

The inclusion of Peeping Tom in the legend of Lady Godiva first appeared in the 17th century. He was supposedly struck blind when he spied on Lady Godiva riding naked through the town. [3]

Far left: Peeping Tom, Hereford Street.

Left: Peeping Tom on the Council House by Henry Wilson and Garrett and Simster.

Right: Godiva Clock, Broadgate. Every hour Lady Godiva moves along a balcony overlooked by Peeping Tom. The accurate clock movement was salvaged from the neglected 100ft Market Tower, which was demolished as part of Coventry's pedestrianisation.

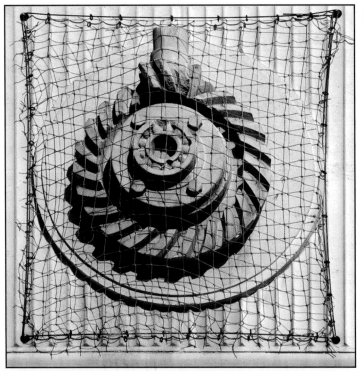

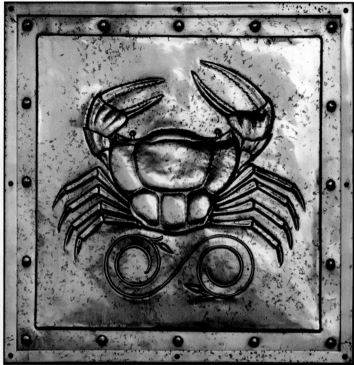

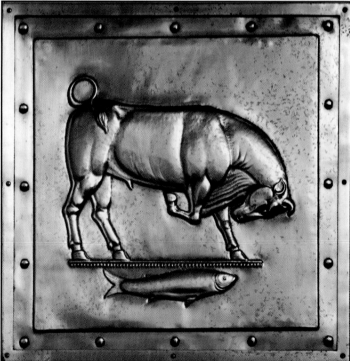

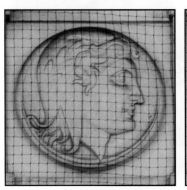
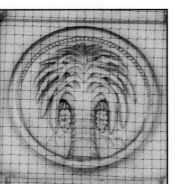
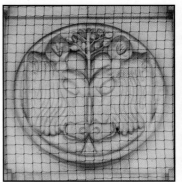
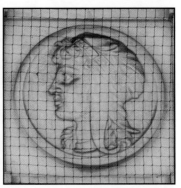

NatWest and Lloyds Banks

The NatWest Bank façade is highly decorated with symbols of Coventry's industry, zodiacal and mythological figures and coins dating from 1930. It was designed by G. & A. Brown, W.F.C. Holden, F.C.R. Palmer and Mr Pearson. Inside is a caduceus above the modern bank counter.

Previous page, left: Symbols of industry on Hereford Street.

Previous page, right: The doors of NatWest Bank showing zodiacal and mythological figures.

Left, top: The inside of Natwest Bank showing the caduceus.

Left, bottom: Coins on the outer façade.

Above: Over the entrance to Lloyds Bank is the symbol of Lloyds, the rearing horse, with two male figures. Unveiled in 1932, the figures may represent Security and Commerce as they are holding a key (security) and a ship (commerce).

The Bull Yard

The Bull Yard in the city centre is named due to its close vicinity of the yard of the now demolished Black Bull Inn, which was one of the largest mediaeval inns in Coventry. The modern Bull Yard was created during post-war development.

Above: The Bull Yard sign against the sky.

Right: *Sir Guy and the Dun Cow* by Alma Ramsey was unveiled between Shelton Square and the Bull Yard in 1952 and shows Sir Guy of Warwick killing the rampaging dun cow to prove his love for the Earl of Warwick's daughter in the upper right of the picture.

Above, left: *Phoenix* by George Wagstaffe represents Coventry's rebirth after World War Two. It was recast in bronze in 1984 after the original, unveiled by Princess Margaret in 1962, became damaged.

Above, right: *Thread Through Time* by R. Corybeare originally had a laser that went up into the sky when it was unveiled in 1998, but this no longer works. The carved and painted cone features scenes from Coventry's history.

Right: These untitled abstract panels by William George Mitchell were positioned on the frontage of the Three Tuns Pub in 1966. The panels can be interpreted as anything from an urban map to an industrial theme of cogs and wheels.

Left: There are 54 of these untitled panels placed along Hertford Street; however, the majority are obscured from the street. There appears to be only one design, and 27 are the same design rotated 180 degrees.

Right: *The People of Coventry*, designed by Trevor Tennant in 1953. These panels, along with another pair, can be found on the back of Broadgate House above Hertford Street and represent Coventry past, present and future. The panel on the left represents creative maturity, and on the right, youth and vitality. The other panels represent the family and planning and working.

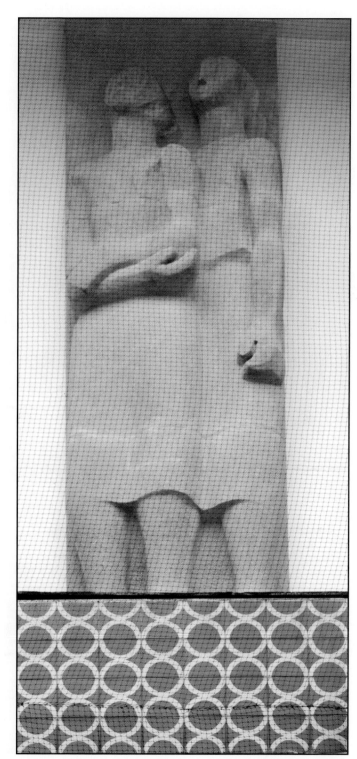

Christchurch Spire

One of the famous three spires of Coventry. The original 13th-century church was built by the Greyfriars Franciscan monks. The spire was retained when the church was demolished as part of the Dissolution of the Monasteries in 1538. A new church was built around the spire in 1832, but this was destroyed in air raids in 1941. In 1950 the ruins were demolished, leaving the spire to stand alone once more.

Far left: The spire against the sky.

Left: The spire is now a café, but the windows are still intact.

Right: There are several bricked up doorways and windows around the spire, most likely due to the destruction of the remainder of the church.

Left: The James Starley Memorial by James Whitehead and Sons. James Starley (1830–1881) is the 'Father of the Bicycle industry'. He formed a company to manufacture sewing machines in Coventry in around 1861, which later began to manufacture French velocipedes. James then began to make his own improvements to the cycles and in 1871 produced the 'Ariel' design, which immensely improved on the French original. [4]

Right, bottom: Details on the James Starley Memorial.

Right, top: The Thomas White Memorial by W.W. Wills and T.W. Wills dates from 1883. Sir Thomas White (d.1566) was a Coventry benefactor, English cloth merchant, founder of St John's College, Oxford and Mayor of London in 1555.

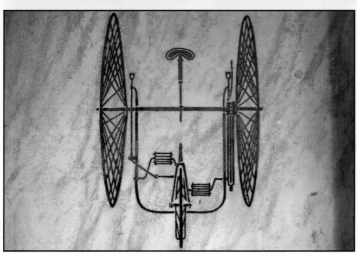

Above: These sculptures of a five-a-side football team, on the roundabout between the ring road and Warwick Road, were created for the International Children's Games in 2005. They were originally red and yellow but have since been painted in Coventry City Football Club colours.

Right: Simon Evans was one of four winners in a council-run competition in 1986 celebrating industry. Originally unveiled in 1986, and situated on the roundabout between the ring road and Warwick Road, *Steel Horse* was restored in 1998 and expresses freedom.

Ford's Hospital

In a backstreet of the modern city, Ford's Hospital is an old almshouse founded in 1509. Fully restored in 1953 after a bomb struck it in 1940, it now contains seven small flats for women. Originally, a chapel connected with the Greyfriars' monastery may have been sited on the same spot.

Above: Gate details looking into the garden of Ford's Hospital.

Right: The exterior of Ford's Hospital.

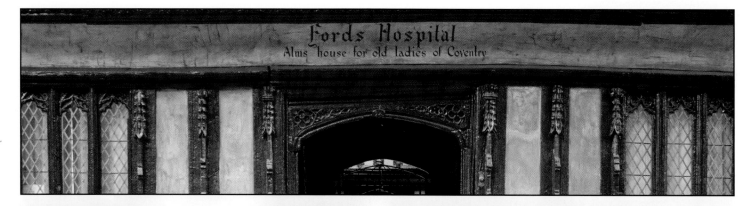

Cheylesmore Manor

Left, top: Writing over the entrance to Ford's Hospital.

Far left, bottom: Ford's Hospital courtyard.

Left: Cheylesmore Manor door.

Above: Cheylesmore Manor.

Hidden from the road is a 13th-century building which was once owned by Queen Isabella. This is the home of Coventry Registry Office and was carefully restored in around 1967 to its current state.

The gatehouse is all that remains of the manor and Edward, the Black Prince, who inherited it from his grandmother in 1338, traditionally used the building as his hunting lodge. [2,5]

CAMERA·PRINCIPIS·

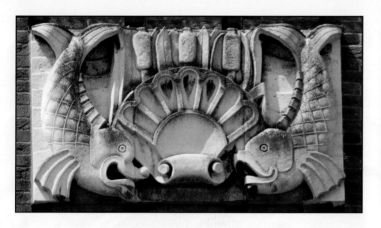

Herbert Art Gallery

Named after Sir Alfred Herbert, a famous Coventry industrialist, the museum and art gallery has several sculptural panels around the exterior of the building.

Left: *City of Coventry Coat of Arms* by A. John Poole is positioned on the south wall of the building.

Right: The panels *Painting, Archaeology, Sculpture, and Natural History* are by Albert Herbert & Son, who were related to Sir Alfred. The city's elephant and castle is in the centre. Positioned on the upper east wall of the museum, the panels were unveiled in 1960.

Previous page: *Man's Struggle.* These two relief panels by Walter Ritchie are situated on the south wall of the Herbert Art Gallery.

The left panel is named *Man's Struggle to Control the World Inside Himself* and depicts ideas such as the past moving into the future and good versus evil. It also contains images relating to death, music, love and women and the Creation.

The right panel is *Man's Struggle to Control the World Outside Himself.* The panel is dominated by a man taming a wild horse and the smaller images include a foetus, a surgeon, workers, a woman reading braille, the pattern of atomic fissure of uranium, a plant and a dividing cell.

Originally designed in 1959, the artwork was moved to its current site in 1994, and there is now an explanatory plaque at its base.

Far left: *Coventry Boy* by Philip Bentham was commissioned by the Coventry Boy Foundation and represents the technical and craft skills within Coventry. It was modelled on a sketch by Reg Rudge and cast by the Singer Morris Foundry.

Left: *The Enfolding* by Jean Parker, completed 1986. Ms Parker was one of four winners in a council-run competition in 1986 celebrating industry.

Above, left: A bronze sculpture of the sculptor Dame Elisabeth Frink, named *Elisabeth Frink*, by F.E. McWilliam, sculpted in a style similar to Dame Frink's own and unveiled in 1966.

Above, right: *Mother and Children* by Gary Galpin, one of the winners in the 1986 Industry competition.

Left: *Basilica* by Paul de Monchaux is positioned so that it varies in appearance depending on the season and the time of day. The stone is from four different quarries and the sculpture has been likened to a judge's wig, which is appropriate with its position near Coventry County Court, which can be seen through it.

Above: Royal coat of arms of the United Kingdom, Coventry County Court.

Whitefriar's Gate and Unknown Mediaeval Ruin

Left: Whitefriar's Gate was built in 1352 as the entrance to Whitefriars monastery, and it later became a toy museum in 1973. This has now closed, and a fire in 2009 destroyed parts of the building.

Right: This structure on Much Park Street remained after the modern parts of the building were burned away in the Blitz, revealing the sandstone beneath. While pottery dating from the 13th to 14th centuries has been found, archaeologists have been unable to discover the building's original purpose, although due to the cellars of the property and its location it is likely to have belonged to a merchant.

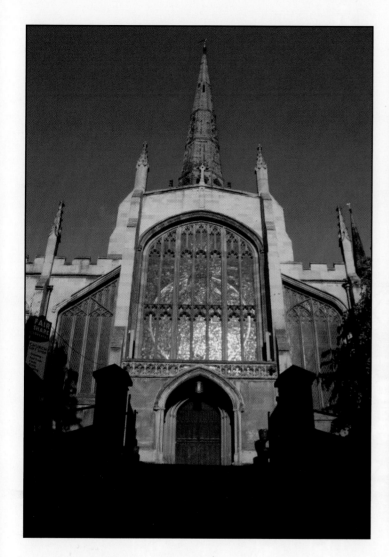

Holy Trinity Church

Holy Trinity Church was built in the early 12th century. The attention to detail within the church is not immediately apparent, but the mediaeval doom painting retains much of its brightness and complexity after extensive restoration. There are also surprises such as the carvings under the rear choir stalls. Holy Trinity was saved in the Blitz from the falling bombs by the vicar (Canon Graham Clitheroe) and a team of firefighters.

Left: Holy Trinity from the St Michael's tower.

Above, left: Holy Trinity from Trinity Lane. You can clearly see the rainbow on the Te Deum Window.

Above, right: The original Victorian West Window was blown out in the Blitz and replaced with Hugh Easton's 1955 Te Deum Window. It shows the history of the church. [6]

Left: The Armorial Window. [6]

Above, left: Detail of the Brides Window and altar. Originally blown out in the Blitz, the current window was designed by Sir Ninian Cooper. The window is so called as couples married in the church after the war donated to the reconstruction. [6]

Above, right: Detail of the candlesticks around the church. Each stick was made by Francis Skidmore and his Coventry company in brass. In the background is the window at the side of the Peace Chapel. [6]

Above: The brass lectern is 15th century and is one of only 33 known to have been cast. The lectern was also used for collecting church funds in the 17th century – money was posted through the beak and collected from the tail. [6]

Right: The 15th-century carved pulpit is supported on a single column and was restored in the 19th century. There are also heads carved in the foliage below the reading desk, which are commonly thought to represent Henry VI and Margaret of Anjou; however, this may be more legend than fact. [6]

Left: The vaulted ceiling of the church is decorated with paintings of angels holding plaques. These contain symbols of the Stations of the Cross, including dice relating to the soldiers casting lots for Jesus's clothing, a chalice, and the Trinity symbol. [7]

Above: The mediaeval doom painting above the Chancel Arch dates from the early 15th century. It was covered over with whitewash after Henry VIII's Reformation before being restored in 1831. It was further restored in 2004.

Left, top: Each of the pew-end carvings within the church is unique and covered with flowers, leaves and vines.

Left, bottom: On the back of the pews there are also small faces carved in intricate detail.

Right: The back of the pews.

Left: The Marler Chapel, also known as the Mercer's Chapel, was added in the early 16th century and was built by a wealthy Coventry merchant named Richard Marler. There is some rich carving in the ceiling, although only at one end, and there are also two carved green men within the chapel. There are still burn marks from a bomb that broke through the ceiling in 1941. [6]

Above: Each of the choir stalls (also known as misericord seats) has a carving underneath it, including shields and this green man. The lip on the top was designed so that the choristers could lean on them during a long service. They are several centuries old and were first sited in Whitefriars, then moved to the Old Grammar School in the city centre before being placed in Holy Trinity. [6]

In Memory of
Mʳ SAMUEL HUNT
Late of this City
and of HANNAH his Wife
He departed this Life
August the 18ᵗʰ 1736
in the 78ᵗʰ year of His Age.
She died November the 6ᵗʰ
1742 Aged 82.
And also of THOˢ HUNT Eſqᵲ
late Alderman of this City
who departed this Life
February the 20ᵀᴴ 1752
Aged 50.

Left: Monuments from other locations in the church have been resited in the Archdeacon's court. Built before 1350, with the roof as old as the 15th century, this was originally used as a church court and for swearing in churchwardens. [6]

Right: This small door may have been a priests' door.

Far right: *The Dove of Peace* was designed by John Clark, a student from Coventry Technical College, and was consecrated in 2001. John has said that it was designed as a Christian symbol and is also a tribute to Sir Frank Whittle and his work in aviation. [8]

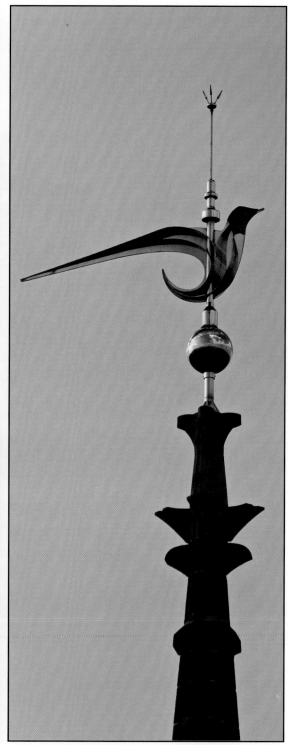

Coventry Cross

The cross near Holy Trinity and the cathedral is a 1960s replica of the original cross. A cross has probably stood in Coventry since the 13th century, although many versions have been erected due to wear and tear. At one point the cross was covered in gold and brightly painted, and the modern version occasionally has small flags held by the gargoyles.

Far left: The cross with the spire of Holy Trinity in the background.

Left: The cross is decorated with images of royalty and mythical beasts.

Right: A unicorn on the cross with St Michael's tower in the background.

Left: *Our Lady of Coventry* in the Prior Gardens by Sister Concordia, a Benedictine nun.

Above: The writing on the Peace Pole by the cathedral means 'May Peace Prevail on Earth' and is repeated around the four sides in Japanese, German, French and English.

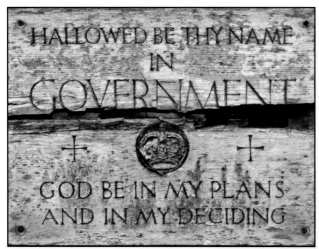

HALLOWED BE THY NAME
IN
GOVERNMENT

GOD BE IN MY PLANS
AND IN MY DECIDING

THE HOME

GOD BE IN MY HEART
AND IN MY LOVING

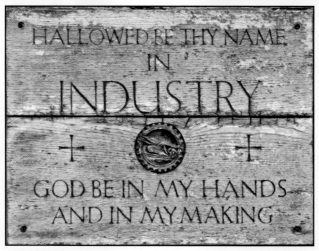

HALLOWED BE THY NAME
IN
INDUSTRY

GOD BE IN MY HANDS
AND IN MY MAKING

HALLOWED BE THY NAME
IN
THE ARTS

GOD BE IN MY SENSES
AND IN MY CREATING

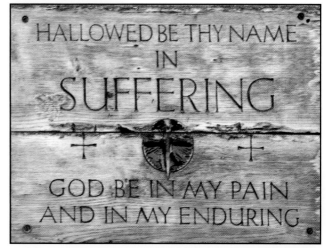

HALLOWED BE THY NAME
IN
SUFFERING

GOD BE IN MY PAIN
AND IN MY ENDURING

Left: These wooden signs on the side of the Georgian House next to the new cathedral echo plaques with the same sayings within the old cathedral.

Right: The stone head on the Georgian House is of unknown origin, but the shape of the mouth and colouration suggests that it may have contained a pipe and been part of a water feature.

The Old Cathedral

There is a wealth of stonework and art that does not get noticed among the grandeur of the old cathedral. During the Coventry Blitz on 14 November 1940 St Michael's was firebombed almost to destruction. Once the fires had died down only the spire, tower, outer wall and bronze effigy of Bishop Yeatman-Briggs, the first bishop of the cathedral, remained.

Left: Details on the outer wall of the cathedral.

Above: The old cathedral at sunset.

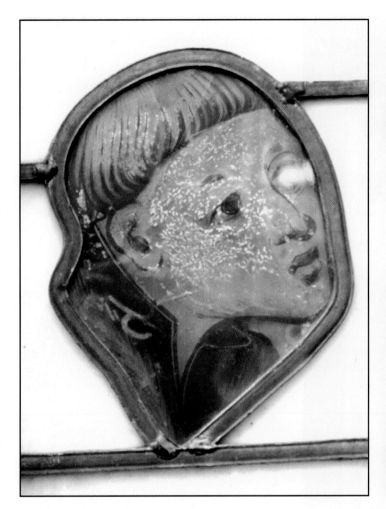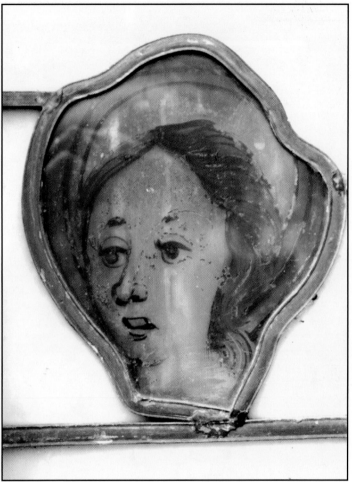

Left: Medallion portraits in the Dyers' Chapel of Dame Mary Bridgeman and Mrs Eliza Samwell, with two coats of arms (one of which contains two red squirrels, the other a lion) underneath them.

Above: This stained glass by John Thornton outside the Bishop Haigh Memorial Chapel, which is also known as the Chapel of the Resurrection, is from the original cathedral windows.

Left: This stone relief by Boulton shows Elizabeth and John the Baptist. It has now lost the brass plaque underneath which commemorated Elizabeth Sarah, wife of Joseph Cash, Jnr, who died in 1863. She was the daughter of Charles Iliffe, whose family later founded the *Coventry Telegraph*.

Right: The skull and crossbones next to the Drapers' Chapel is a common mortality symbol. It can also be found on the exterior of the cathedral.

Previous page, left: The view from the top of St Michael's tower.

Previous page, centre: *Christ* was originally created by a pupil of Blundell's school in Devon, Alain John, at the age of 18. It was recast in bronze in around 1944 for Coventry after his death at the age of 23. He was an RAF navigator and the statue is a memorial for those who lost their lives in the war.

Previous page, right: *Ecco Homo* by Sir Jacob Epstein was carved during 1934–35 from a block of Subiaco marble. Given to Coventry Cathedral at the wish of Lady Epstein, it was dedicated on 22 March 1969. The statue shows Christ before Pilate.

Above: Around the outside of the old cathedral are many carvings of religious and royal figures, as well as these carvings on the Bayley Lane side of the ruins. Sadly the head on the right has suffered some damage from a lorry passing along the lane.

Bishop Huyshe Wolcott Yeatman-Biggs

Bishop Yeatman-Biggs was the first Bishop of the restored See of Coventry when St Michael's became a cathedral in 1918. One of the few items remaining after the bombing of the cathedral, this bronze, originally designed for the interior, had been unveiled in 1925.

Left: The sculpture of Bishop Yeatman-Biggs has a swastika on the mitre which was originally a symbol of peace.

Below: The sculpture is holding a model showing what the cathedral originally looked like. One of the hands was severed in the Blitz, but has since been restored.

Reconciliation by Josefina de Vasconcellos was originally sculpted in 1977. In 1995, to mark the 50th anniversary of the end of World War Two, a bronze cast was placed in the ruins of St Michael's. The original is sited in front of Bradford University library, and further casts are in Japan, Belfast and Berlin. It was originally named *Reunion*, and renamed at the request of Bradford's Peace Studies department when it was re-unveiled in 1994. [9]

Previous page, left: Door detail on St Michael's tower.

Previous page, right: Grotesques on St Michael's tower door.

Opposite page, left: The West Window with engravings of angels and saints by John Hutton seen through a door of the old cathedral. It links the two buldings with the reflection of the old in the new.

Opposite page, right: Detail of the West Window.

Above: The St Chad's cross on the north side of the cathedral is echoed in the cross on top of the Chapel of Industry. The cross also appears on the arms of the diocese. [10]

Left: Cherub door handles by Jacob Epstein. Originally designed in 1956, these are a second cast given to the cathedral after his death.

The New Cathedral

The decision to build the new St Michael's Cathedral was made the day after the old one had been destroyed. Initially, Sir Giles Gilbert Scott was asked to design the new cathedral and submitted his design in 1944; however the Royal Fine Arts Commission rejected his submission and Sir Basil Spence won the competition held in 1950 to find a new design. The new building is untraditional and modern, but is designed to work with the old traditional cathedral to form a whole. The foundation stone was laid by Queen Elizabeth II in 1956, and the cathedral was consecrated in 1962.

Above: In alcoves around the cathedral are these stained-glass windows, which you can see looking back from the altar. They represent the artists' impressions of Creation through to Adam and Eve, overcoming temptation, death and sorrow and then finally Heaven. [11]

Right: The Baptistry window was designed by John Piper. About 25m high, it contains around 200 stained-glass panes crafted by Patrick Reyntiens. [12]

Left: The symbol of the Holy Spirit on a wooden crown of thorns by Elisabeth Frink, in front of Graham Sutherland's *Great Tapestry*, which shows Christ in majesty surrounded by various Christian symbols.

Right: Elisabeth Frink designed the bronze eagle on the bronze and aformosia pulpit and lectern. [13]

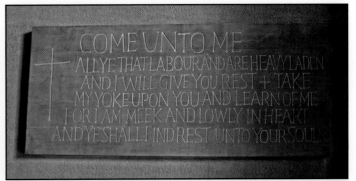

COME UNTO ME
ALL YE THAT LABOUR AND ARE HEAVY LADEN
AND I WILL GIVE YOU REST + TAKE
MY YOKE UPON YOU AND LEARN OF ME
FOR I AM MEEK AND LOWLY IN HEART
AND YE SHALL FIND REST UNTO YOUR SOUL

A NEW COMMANDMENT
I GIVE UNTO YOU + THAT
YE LOVE ONE ANOTHER
AS I HAVE LOVED YOU

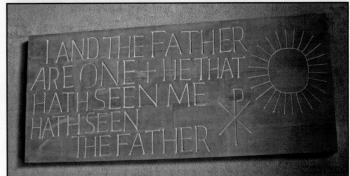

I AND THE FATHER
ARE ONE + HE THAT
HATH SEEN ME
HATH SEEN
THE FATHER

Left, top: The High Altar cross made by Geoffrey Clark holds the original cross of nails made from three mediaeval nails from the roof of the old cathedral and represents a phoenix rising from the ashes. It was presented to the cathedral by the Worshipful Company of Goldsmiths. [14, 15]

Left, bottom: Marking the route that clergy and the choir progress down the central aisle are two rows of 1962 pennies embedded in the floor. The cathedral was consecrated in 1962, and several are unreadable from the feet that have rubbed them smooth over the years.

Above, left: *The Stalingrad Madonna* in the Millennium Chapel is a copy of a sketch drawn by Kurt Reuber, a German solider, in 1942. There are also copies in Berlin and Stalingrad (now Volgograd). [16]

Above, right: *Tablets of the Word* by Ralph Beyer are eight plaques at various positions around the cathedral with Christian quotes on.

Left: *The Swedish Windows* by Einar Forseth.

Right: The symbol of Aktion Sühnezeichen Friedensdienste (Action for Reconciliation and Peace) was presented to the cathedral in 1961. A team from ASF, a German organisation, built the International Centre in the ruins of the cathedral. [17]

Left: The ceiling of the cathedral is a work of art in itself. Made of Canadian spruce, the ceiling can be 'tuned' for different events depending on the acoustics required. [18]

Right: *The Peace Bell* was a gift from Germany on the 50th anniversary of the Coventry air raid. 'Peace' is written in both English and German (*Friede*) around the waist of the bell. [19]

Above: *The Plumbline and the City* by Clarke Fitz-Gerald is a sculpture based on Amos 7:7,8, and represents God judging a city and its citizens. It was presented to the cathedral in 1971. [20]

Left: Chair backs depicting the coat of arms of Coventry and the royal coat of arms of the United Kingdom

Right: The floor of the Unity Chapel was created by Einar Forseth and donated by Sweden. The windows surrounding the chapel were donated by Germany and are by Margaret Traherne. [21]

Previous page, left: The mosaic of the Angel in the Chapel of Christ in Gethsemane is by Steven Sykes. He also created the panel to the left of the mosaic which shows the disciples sleeping in the garden. The crown of thorns surrounding the chapel from the outside was designed by Basil Spence and crafted by the Royal Engineers. [22]

Previous page, right: Looking up at the *Crown of Thorns* by Geoffrey Clarke and cross from the altar in the Chapel of Christ the Servant, also known as the Chapel of Industry. The cross and altar were presented by Coventry apprentices. [23]

Left: *Christ Crucified* by Helen Huntington Jennings was sculpted from the wreckage of a crashed car.

Right: The *Czech Cross* was a gift from its maker, Jindrich Severa.

Left: 22 Bayley Lane is a Tudor house around 500 years old and the only one remaining in a row of cottages. Originally there was an extension between the building and the Guildhall next door.

Above: Foliate carvings on the façade of the building.

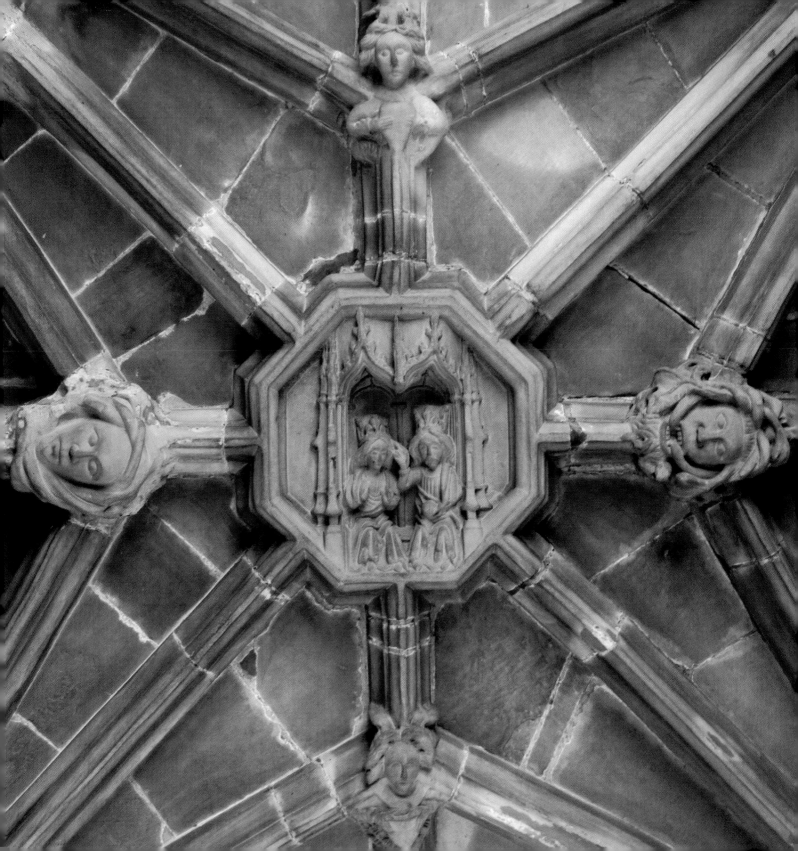

St Mary's Guildhall

The Guildhall began to be built around 1340 and was originally the guildhall and chambers for the merchant guilds of St Mary and Holy Trinity. [24]

The hall is strongly connected to King Henry VI and Mary, Queen of Scots, was also held within the Guildhall for a day and a night before being moved.

William Shakespeare also performed in the Great Hall, and one of the faces on the old cathedral strongly resembles him.

Left: The boss under the gateway into the Guildhall. On the right you can see a green man, and in the centre is a representation known as the Coronation of the Virgin Mary.

Right: This Cumbrian sandstone statue of two minstrels by Michael Disley is sited in the courtyard of the Guildhall. It was funded by the European Regional Development Fund.

Left: *Lady Godiva* by W.C. Marshall sits in the late 15th-century oriel window and was sculpted in the mid-19th century. [25]

Right, top: The great hall of the Guildhall looking up to the minstrels' gallery.

Right, bottom: Detail on the oriel window showing people working. The one on the left probably reads 'and with my sickle'.

Far left: The ceiling in the Guildhall has been fully restored after being partially destroyed in the Blitz. One of the angels in the ceiling has the original wings, but the rest have been replaced.

Left: The Prince's Chamber is covered in rich carvings, including this fireplace. The room is named after the city motto, 'Camera Principis'.

Left: The window in the Draper's Room shows the cat-a-mountain, a symbol of watchfulness, abo Coventry's elephant and castle and the motto of Coventry.

Right: The Great North Window contains coats of arms and portraits of previous kings of Engla both real and fictional, including Arthur, Henry VI and Edward.

Left: The Great Chair in the Old Council Chamber, which probably dates from around the late 14th century or early 15th century, has a wealth of detail that is often in shadow; however, if you look closely you can make out the figure of the Virgin and Child. It has been used by James I, James II and possibly Elizabeth I. [25]

Right, top: The top of one of the chairs in the Old Council Chamber has Coventry's symbol of the elephant and castle carved into it.

Right, bottom: These faces are usually in shadow; however, they are beautifully carved reliefs of male and female profiles.

Left: Detail on the treasure chest in the Treasury. This appears to be pre-13th century. [25]

Right: These religious-themed reliefs behind glass in the Treasury are backed on cork. Dating from around 1400, they were moved from the Benedictine Priory guest house to the Guildhall in 1832. Originally displayed on the ceiling of the Old Council Chamber, the central figure represents God and there are also figures of Mary and the child Jesus, John the Baptist, St Catherine and St Michael, as well as an eagle and an angel. [25]

Above, left: *The Dudley Plaque* next to the Draper's Room is made of bronze and dates from the Elizabethan era, confirming the Dudley family's charitable grant of land. [25]

Above, right: The door handle on the Treasury door is a detail often missed.

Above, left: A halberd displayed on the minstrel's gallery is one of the surviving pieces of the city's armoury, originally stored in the Armoury. [25]

Above, right: *The Coventry Cloth of Gold* by Janet Stoyel was installed in the ante room in 2001.

Left: This is a copy of the 15th-century sculpture of St George. The sculpture was originally in St George's chapel, which was demolished in the 19th century. The original is now in the Herbert Museum. There is also a tradition that St George was born in Coventry. [25] [26]

Right: *Lady Godiva* by William Behnes sits above the fireplace in the Draper's Room.

Above, left: Decoration in a Greek revival style on the Draper's Hall.

Above, right: The County Hall, or County Court, dates from when Coventry was a county in its own right. Cuckoo Lane, which runs alongside the building, was the site of the last public execution in Coventry in 1849. [27]

Above: The three 17th-century Lychgate cottages were originally one house constructed by Revd Bryan of Holy Trinity. They were built using reclaimed timbers from Spon Street, which had been stored in the church yard and have been dated to the 15th century. The cottages are named after the roofed porches situated at entrances to graveyards; a funeral procession would bring the corpse (or lych) to the gate, where they would wait for the priest.

Previous page: Details on the Flying Standard pub show Lady Godiva, the three spires and the elephant and castle.

Above, left: *Waterwindow* by Susanna Heron is positioned on one side of the Priory Cloister Garden.

Above right, top: This carving is situated over an entrance to the old Blue Coat School, founded in 1714. It is now the Holy Trinity Church Centre.

Above right, bottom: This carved lettering marks where the Priory Mill water is thought to have flowed. [28]

Cofa's Tree

The Anglo-Saxon origin of the name of the city of Coventry is thought to be 'Cofantreo' or 'Cofa's Tree'. The city was once in the Forest of Arden, and it may have come from a tree there, potentially on the boundary of land belonging to a person named Cofa. It has also been suggested that the tree stood in Broadgate. Another idea is that it is derived from 'Couaentree', where 'couaen' (also spelt as 'cune') means a meeting place of waters. The Radford Brook used to meet with the River Sherbourne (also known as the Cune) in the city centre.

Above, left: *Cofa's Tree* by Chris Brown is in the Priory Gardens and was made partly from pieces found during the excavation of the old St Mary's Priory. [28]

Above, right: Tower on the top of the old Blue Coat School.

The Undercroft

The Undercroft next to Millennium Place houses the remains of St Mary's Cathedral and Benedictine Priory, the original cathedral of Coventry. Construction began in the early 12th century and the priory was demolished during Henry VIII's Dissolution of the Monasteries. [29]

Left: The walls of the undercroft are well preserved, and the statues of the Benedictine monks give you an insight into how the priory used to look.

Right: This modern lapidary wall is studded with examples of stonework across the ages. A few of them have makers' marks carved into them.

Frank Whittle and the Whittle Arch

Sir Frank Whittle was an RAF officer who invented the jet engine. Born in 1907 in Coventry, he died in 1996.

Left: The 2007 statue *Sir Frank Whittle* by Faith Winter is situated in Millennium Place with the wing-like structure of the Whittle Arch soaring above.

Right: The *Whittle Arch* at night is brightly lit.

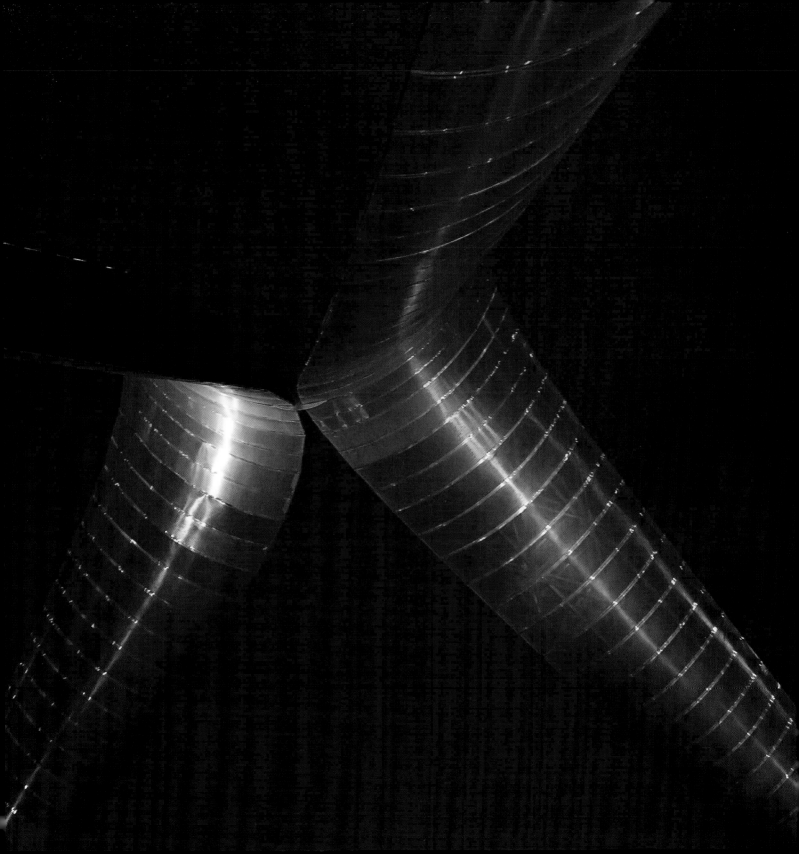

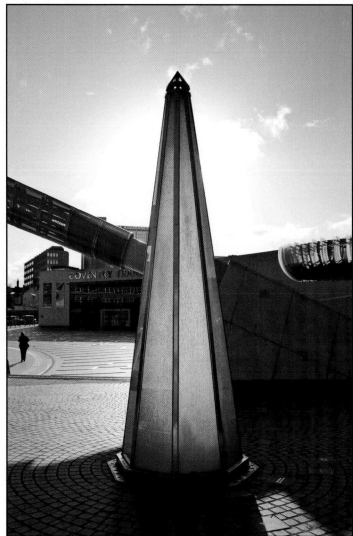

Above, left: *Unity* was a project by various groups in Hillfields.

Above, right: *The Future Monument* by Jochen Gerz.

Right: The *Glass Bridge* circles 360 degrees from Coventry Transport Museum over Lady Herbert's Garden to The Garden of International Friendship. Beneath it is the *Millennium Clock* by Françoise Schein; the blue lines represent the time-zones of the world.

Left: The *Glass Bridge* over Millennium Place with the Swanswell Gate in the background shows the new against the old.

Lady Herbert's Garden

In the early 1930s Sir Alfred Herbert laid out this garden in memory of his wife, Florence, who had died unexpectedly.

The garden lies between Cook Street and the Cook Street Gate, and Swanswell Gate, and contains the Old Rope Walk running along the side of the section of the old city wall which remains in the garden.

Left: The *Glass Bridge* over the garden.

Right, top: The signs at the entrances to the garden.

Right: Detailed gate posts on the way into the garden.

Far right: The Arts and Crafts pergola was designed between 1935 and 1937 and represents the four seasons. It also once had decoration relevant to the seasons around the building.

LADY HERBERT'S GARDEN

135

Left: The door and lamp on Swanswell Gate, one of the two remaining original gates. It is also known as Priory Gate.

Far left: Detail on the gate to Lady Herbert's Garden, with Florence Herbert's initials among the metalwork.

Left: The fence posts surrounding the garden all have Lady Herbert's initials in these detailed heads.

139

Above, left and right: Gargoyles on the Swanswell Gate.

Right: Gargoyle on the Cook Street Gate.

Right: The weathervane on the top of the Swanswell Gate has Florence Herbert's initials in the flag.

Above, left: A side street off the Burges towards Palmer Lane is a reminder of the old Coventry.

Above, right: The River Sherbourne now runs under the modern city. This section next to Palmer Lane is the only visible place in the city centre where the river rises to the surface.

Right: *Rebuilding Coventry and the Co-op's Activities* by John Skelton are a series of 1956 carvings on columns outside the Co-op building on Corporation Street. They show ideas such as holidays for employees, industry, and flower seeds and nursery supply, as well as others.

Left: The *Bryan Bailey Memorial* by Norelle Keddie shows a small figure between the traditional comic and tragic theatre masks. Bryan was a director at the Belgrade theatre and, following his death in a road accident in 1960, the sculpture was commissioned by Bryan's mother and unveiled in 1962.

Above: *Belgrade* by James C. Brown depicts the city of Belgrade as a fortress on a hill surrounded by the Danube with the city arms and the city name at the top. The theatre was named after the city as a mark of friendship and Yugoslavia also supplied timber for the interior of the building.

Above: Bablake Old Boys' Club on Spon Street.

Right: The carved *c.*16th-century arch contains the Coventry coat of arms in the centre with a lion or dragon on the left and on the right a chequered chevron and three stars.

Above, left: This shaft in the centre of the courtyard of old Bablake School and Bond's Hospital is of unknown origin, but it is likely to mark the place where the old water pump was sited. The shaft is decorated with gothic motifs.

Above, right: The back of Bond's Hospital, which is an almshouse founded in 1506 by Thomas Bond, a former Mayor of Coventry.

Above: Bablake School was founded in around 1560 and heavily funded by Thomas Wheatley, a previous Mayor of Coventry. The Bablake land was given in 1344 by Queen Isabella, and the school itself could date from then.

Church of St John the Baptist

Founded by Queen Isabella in 1330, St John's chapel was dedicated in 1350, and the church was expanded over the years.

The church fell into neglect in 1660; however, in 1734 the church was restored as a parish church. Much restoration work has been done over the years, but there is still a wealth of detail around the church.

The phrase 'sent to Coventry' is traditionally thought to have originated from the church being used to imprison Royalist soldiers in 1647 during the Civil War. They were then ignored by the local people, who supported parliment. [2, 30]

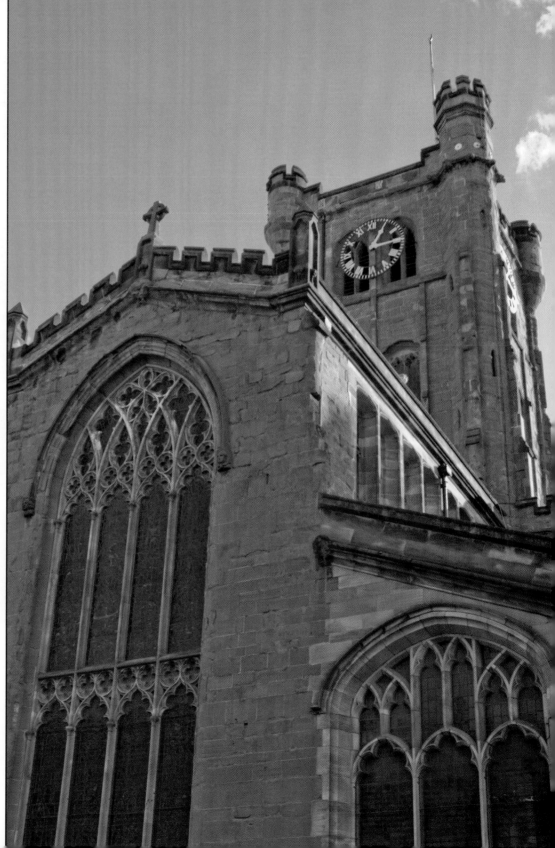

Far left: Carvings around the exterior doors of the entrance.

Left: Exterior view of the church.

Above: Interior of the church.

Right: The altar and East Window.

Right: The lectern is carved with detailed wooden models of the four Christian gospel symbols. The lion is St Mark's symbol, with the winged man of St Matthew in the background. On the other sides are the winged ox of St Luke and the eagle of St John.

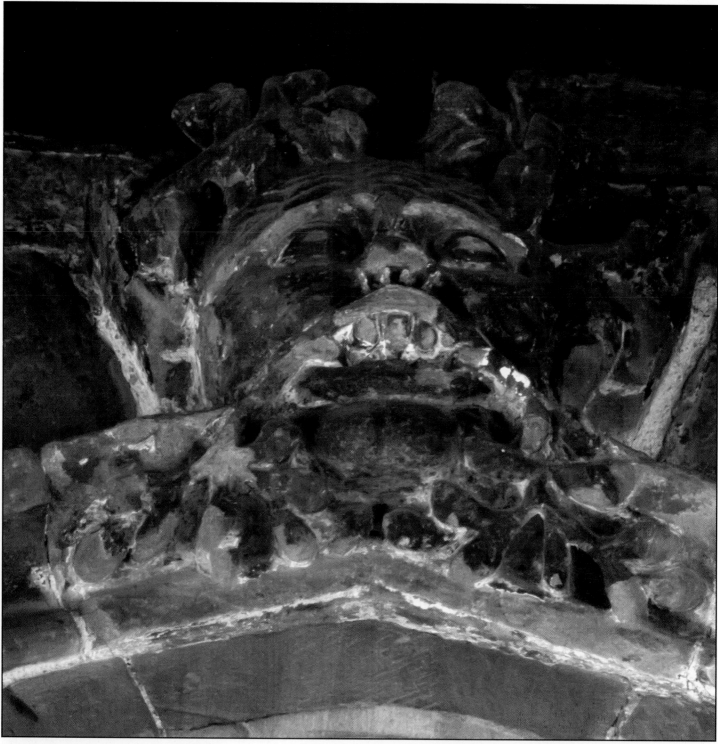

Left: This green man above the West Window is hidden in the rafters of the church and it is unusual as it appears to have teeth. A green man is recognisable by the leaves pouring from its mouth, and you can also see the crown of leaves around the head.

Above: This detailed carving near the ceiling also contains a green man, top right.

Right: Two of the Stations of the Cross that are sited around the church.

Above: A side altar in the church.

Right: Candle against the pulpit.

Far right: A statue of the Madonna and Child with votive candles beneath.

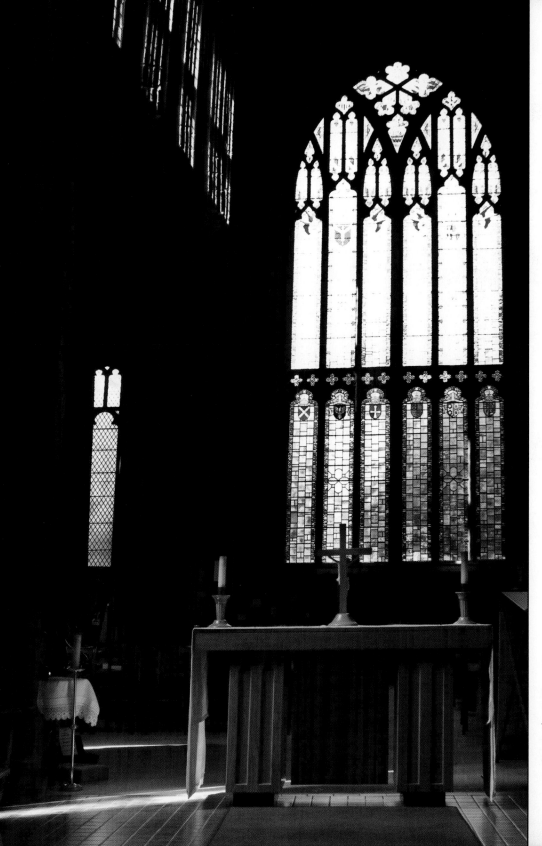

Left: The West Window.

Right: This stained-glass window showing St John the Baptist also contains, from left to right, the wheel of St Catherine, St Chad's Cross[10], the Coventry elephant and castle, and the coat of arms of Edward III.

ECCE AGNUS DEI

Saint John the Baptist

REMEMBER BEFORE GOD BARBARA ANN WEAVER.
WHO WORSHIPPED HERE AND DEPARTED THIS LIFE
6TH NOVEMBER 1951. THIS WINDOW WAS ERECTED
BY HER SON WILLIAM ARTHUR WEAVER.

Left: Floor tiles at the West Window.

Right: The organ.

Far right: The exterior of the church has detailed stone carvings, including St John the Baptist, wearing a camelskin and holding a cross with a banner appearing to say 'repent'.

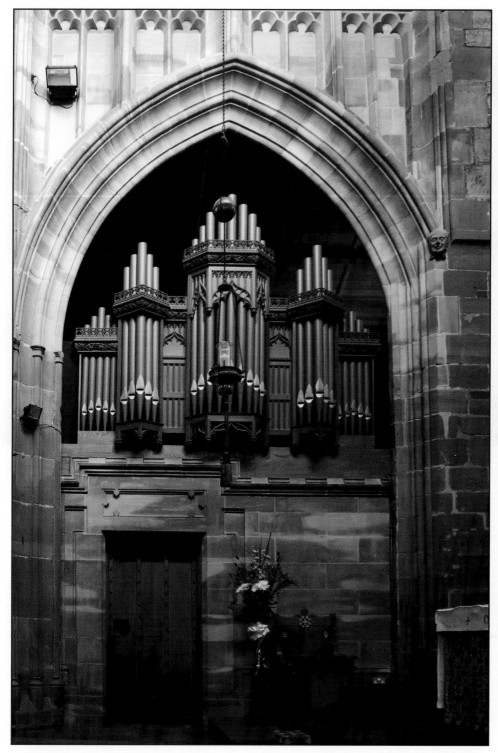

Spon Street

Spon Street is made up partly of ancient timber buildings moved from other locations where they would otherwise have been demolished. For example, No. 9 originally stood in Much Park Street. The name Spon probably comes from the wood of Spon (or Spanna) mentioned in a 13th-century document.

Above: A jettied bay on 20–21 Spon Street.

Right: The frontage on 20–21 Spon Street is approximately 16th century. The building was originally located on Much Park Street and was known as the Green Dragon Inn. [2, 31]

164

Left: The rear of No. 2 Spon Street, which was moved to the street in 1989.

Above, left: A door in Spon Street, which fits in perfectly with the style of the street.

Above, right: A window at the far end of Spon Street above Nos 161–162. This is an example of a Wealden-style house.

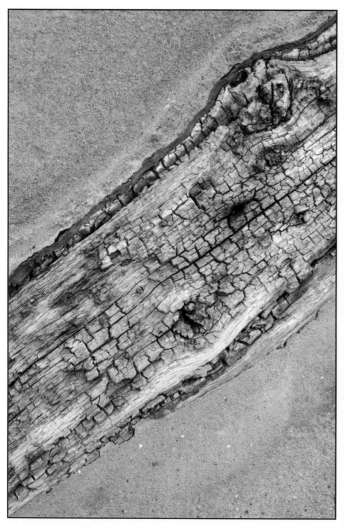

Above: Wooden decoration on the exterior of one of the Spon Street buildings.

Right: The Weavers House on Upper Spon Street dates from 1455 and after the Dissolution of the Monasteries passed from the Priory to the Mercers' Guild. The building has been restored today to how it would have looked in 1540 when a weaver occupied it. [32]

St James and St Christopher's

The ruins of this 14th-century wayfarer's chapel sit next to the bridge over the River Sherbourne in Spon End. Dedicated in the 15th century to saints associated with ferrymen and travellers, the building eventually became a house. The council proposed that it was restored in 1936, but when it suffered slight bomb damage in World War Two it was dismantled and left as a ruin in 1952. [33]

Above: The chapel from the Spon Bridge. This end of the city may be where tanners and dyers operated, due to their need to be near running water, which was plentiful from the River Sherbourne. It was also on the edge of the city, so the fumes from the trades did not reach into the city centre. [34]

Right: Looking through the ruins.

Whitefriars Friary

This is just a small part of the friary lands, the mediaeval cloister wing – Whitefriar's Gate was also part of the grounds. When Henry VIII disbanded religious communities in the early 16th century the estate was sold, and eventually the friary became owned by John Hales, who founded the King Henry VIII School. The building became a workhouse in 1801 until the end of World War Two and is now closed.

Left: Queen Elizabeth I stayed in the property and addressed the people of Coventry from this oriel window in 1565.

Above: The remaining building by the ring road looks out of place entering the modern city.

Right: The intricate stonework above this doorway can still be seen.

Canal Basin

Just outside the ring road lies Coventry Canal Basin. Built in the 1760s, the canal basin is now lined with small shops as well as being a working canal. The old warehouses are also still visible.

Left: The bridge over the ring road clearly signposts the location of the canal basin, which is not obvious from the exterior due to the warehouses surrounding it.

Above: Two of the canal boats moored at the basin.

Far left: *James Brindley* by James Walter Butler was unveiled in 1998 and shows him looking at drawings in the direction of a bridge that he built along the canal. James Brindley was an engineer in the 18th century who worked on the Grand Canal, as well as the Chesterfield and Birmingham canals and others. In the 1760s he worked on Coventry Canal Basin.

Left: A Coventry Canal Society sign that points the boats down the canal.

Right: *City Basin Mosaic* by Rosalind Wates dates from 1997 and depicts the canal, the basin and symbols of Coventry.

Left: Various details around the canal basin, including cogs on a crane, a mooring bollard and a cycle rack.

Right: *Lock Gates* by Ondre Nowakowski sits near the Foleshill Road roundabout. Unveiled in 1997, it is made of oak and apparently includes the silouette of a house.

Coventry Martyrs Memorial

The Coventry Martyrs Memorial near the ring road was created by G. Maile and Sons and represents the Lollard Martyrs. The Lollards were a 15th-century religious movement who followed John Wycliffe's beliefs, and in the early 16th century people were burned at the stake at Park Hollows. The memorial was later moved to its current position. [35]

Left: The wheel-head Celtic cross against the sun.

Below: The cross sits on a stepped platform with the Coventry coat of arms and a wreath on the front.

Camera Principis and the Elephant and Castle

As you walk around Coventry, the motto and symbol of the city is repeated around the city.

Camera Principis is the motto of Coventry; it means 'The Prince's Chamber'. This is traditionally thought to refer to Edward, the Black Prince, and his close ties to the city.

The golden elephant and three-turreted castle coat of arms dates from at least early mediaeval times. It possibly refers to the strength of the elephant, and its ability to carry a castle on its back – the castle itself being a symbol of strength. The cat-a-mountain over the crest is a symbol of watchfulness.

The crest today includes the black eagle of Earl Leofric and a phoenix rising from the ashes symbolising the resurrection of Coventry after World War Two. These were added in 1959. [2, 36]

Previous page: Phoenix and Elephant bollards outside Cathedral Lanes.

Right: This window in St John the Baptist's church shows the English coat of arms summounted by a lion and is connected with the Black Prince. [37]

Far right: This old elephant and castle in Coventry is the boss on the underside of the Cook Street gate and retains a remarkable amount of colour for its age.

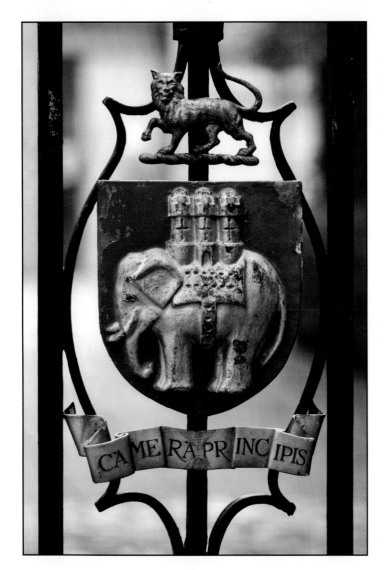

Above, left: An elephant and castle on gates between 22 Bayley Lane and St Mary's Guildhall.

Above, right: An elephant and castle with the Coventry Civic Sword and Mace on the gates on the Council House.

Opposite page, left: The Coventry elephant and castle on the Martyrs Memorial near the ring road.

Opposite page, right: These bollards can be found throughout the city and are topped by an elephant.

Page 192

Top left: There are several bollards around the city with the coat of arms and motto on the side in silver.

Top right: The carpet in St Mary's Guildhall is covered with the Coventry coat of arms.

Bottom left: Unveiled in 1958, this coat of arms on the Belgrade Theatre was designed by James C. Brown and made by Edward Grey of G. Lister and Sons, Cambridge.

Bottom right: This elephant and castle can be found in St Mary's Guildhall in the oriel window, beneath the statue of Lady Godiva.

References

The following sources are the primary references used throughout this book:

1   Public Monuments and Sculpture Association [Online] (URL http://www.pmsa.org.uk/), accessed August 2009.
2   Robert Orland, Historic Coventry [Online] (URL http://www.historiccoventry.co.uk), accessed August 2009.

The following pages have also been referenced:

3   Peter Barton, The Coventry Pages, Peeping Tom [Online] (URL http://www.thecoventrypages.net/section.asp?catid=76), accessed August 2009.
4   Coventry Transport Museum Wiki [Online] (http://wiki.transport-museum.com/James%20Starley.ashx), accessed August 2009.
5   Peter Barton, The Coventry Pages, Cheylesmore Manor House [Online] (URL http://www.thecoventrypages.net/section.asp?catid=98), accessed August 2009.
6   Take-A-Pew Virtual Tour [Online] (URL http://take-a-pew.org.uk/virtual.html), accessed August 2009.
7   Take-A-Pew Stations of the Cross [Online] (URL http://take-a-pew.org.uk/stationsofthecross.html), accessed August 2009.
8   Take-A-Pew Dove of Peace [Online] (URL http://take-a-pew.org.uk/doveofpeace.html), accessed August 2009
9   Bradford University, Sculptor Unveils 'Reconciliation' [Online] (URL http://www.brad.ac.uk/university/newsandviews/94-11/sculptor_unveils_reconciliation.html), accessed August 2009.
10 Seiyaku.com [Online] (URL http://www.seiyaku.com/customs/crosses/chad.html), accessed August 2009.
11 Coventry Cathedral Virtual Tour, South Nave [Online] (URL http://coventrycathedraltour.org.uk/node.php?n=south_nave), accessed August 2009.
12 Peter Barton, The Coventry Pages, Baptistery Window and Font [Online] (URL http://www.thecoventrypages.net/section.asp?catid=174), accessed August 2009.
13 Peter Barton, The Coventry Pages, The Lectern [Online] (URL http://www.thecoventrypages.net/section.asp?catid=182), accessed August 2009.
14 Peter Barton, The Coventry Pages, The Altar [Online] (URL http://www.thecoventrypages.net/section.asp?catid=180), accessed August 2009.
15 Coventry Cathedral Virtual Tour, High Altar Cross [Online] (URL http://coventrycathedraltour.org.uk/node.php?n=high_altar_cross), accessed August 2009
16 Coventry Cathedral Virtual Tour, Millenium Chapel [Online] (URL http://coventrycathedraltour.org.uk/node.php?n=millennium_chapel), accessed August 2009.
17 Coventry Cathedral Virtual Tour, Swedish Window [Online] (URL http://coventrycathedraltour.org.uk/node.php?n=swedish_window#), accessed August 2009.
18 Peter Barton, The Coventry Pages, Details around the Cathedral [Online] (URL http://www.thecoventrypages.net/section.asp?catid=184), accessed August 2009.
19 Coventry Cathedral Virtual Tour, North Nave [Online] (URL http://coventrycathedraltour.org.uk/node.php?n=north_nave), accessed August 2009.
20 Coventry Cathedral Signage.
21 Coventry Cathedral Virtual Tour, Chapel of Unity [Online] (URL http://coventrycathedraltour.org.uk/node.php?n=chapel_of_unity), accessed August 2009.
22 Coventry Cathedral Virtual Tour, Christ in Gethsemane [Online] (URL http://coventrycathedraltour.org.uk/node.php?n=christ_in_gethsemane), accessed August 2009.
23 Peter Barton, The Coventry Pages, Chapel of Christ the Servant [Online] (URL http://www.thecoventrypages.net/section.asp?catid=177) Accessed August 2009.
24 George Demidowicz, Coventry City Council plaques.
25 St Mary's Guildhall Information Leaflets, Coventry City Council and knowledge from David McGrory (local historian) and Leigh Moor (Blue Badge Tourist Guide) (August 2009).
26 Peter Barton, The Coventry Pages, St Mary's Hall [Online] (URL http://www.thecoventrypages.net/section.asp?catid=95), accessed August 2009.
27 Peter Barton, The Coventry Pages, County Hall [Online] (URL http://www.thecoventrypages.net/section.asp?catid=105), accessed August 2009.
28 CABE - Phoenix Initiative [Online] (URL http://www.cabe.org.uk/case-studies/phoenix-initiative/description), accessed August 2009.
29 Peter Barton, The Coventry Pages, St Mary's Cathedral - the First Cathedral [Online] (URL http://www.thecoventrypages.net/section.asp?catid=51), accessed August 2009.
30 Peter Barton, The Coventry Pages, St John's Bablake - sent to Coventry [Online] (URL http://www.thecoventrypages.net/section.asp?catid=94), accessed August 2009.
31 Spon Street external sign on building.
32 Spon End Building Preservation Trust, The Weaver's House [Online] (URL http://www.sebpt.org.uk/), accessed August 2009.
33 Peter Ward (http://ourwardfamily.com/our_family_roots.htm)
34 Peter Barton, The Coventry Pages, Spon End [Online] (URL http://www.thecoventrypages.net/section.asp?catid=113), accessed August 2009.
35 Peter Barton, The Coventry Pages, Coventry Martyrs [Online] (URL http://www.thecoventrypages.net/section.asp?catid=103), accessed August 2009.
36 Coventry City Council: Coat of Arms – the Armorial Bearings of the City of Coventry [Online] (http://www.coventry.gov.uk/ccm/content/legal-%26-democratic-services-directorate/democratic-services/lord-mayors/coat-of-arms---the-armorial-bearings-of-the-city-of-coventry.en), accessed August 2009.
37 Peter Barton, The Coventry Pages, The Black Prince [Online] (URL http://www.thecoventrypages.net/section.asp?catid=92), accessed August 2009.

Bibliography

The following sites have been used as sources for this book, or have provided assistance:

Bradford University
http://www.brad.ac.uk/university/newsandviews/94-11/sculptor_unveils_reconciliation.html

CABE – Phoenix Initiative
http://www.cabe.org.uk/case-studies/phoenix-initiative/description

Coventry Cathedral
http://coventrycathedral.org.uk

Coventry Cathedral Virtual Tour,
http://coventrycathedraltour.org.uk

Coventry City Council, St Mary's Guildhall
www.coventry.gov.uk/stmarys

Coventry Transport Museum Wiki
http://wiki.transport-museum.com

Historic Coventry
http://www.historiccoventry.co.uk

Holy Trinity Coventry
http://www.holytrinitycoventry.org.uk/

Our Family Roots
http://ourwardfamily.com/

Seiyaku.com
http://www.seiyaku.com

Spon End Building Preservation Trust
http://www.sebpt.org.uk/

St John The Baptist
http://www.stjohn-the-baptist.co.uk/

Take-A-Pew
http://take-a-pew.org.uk

The Coventry Pages
http://www.thecoventrypages.net

The Public Monuments and Sculpture Association
http://www.pmsa.org.uk/

Wikipedia
http://en.wikipedia.org/